Time Goes By

A Year at a
Construction
Site

Nicholas Harris

M Millbrook Press / Minneapolis

First American edition published in 2009 by Lerner Publishing Group, Inc.

Copyright © 2004 by Orpheus Books Ltd.

Millbrook Press
A division of Lerner Publishing Group, Inc.
241 First Avenue North
Minneapolis, MN 55401 USA

Website address: www.lernerbooks.com

Library of Congress Cataloging-in-Publication Data

Harris, Nicholas, 1956–
    A year at a construction site / by Nicholas Harris.
        p.   cm. -- (Time goes by)
    Includes bibliographical references.
        ISBN 978–1–58013–549–8 (lib. bdg. : alk. paper)
    1. Building—Juvenile literature. 2. School buildings—Design and construction—Juvenile literature. I. Title.
TH149.H37 2009
    690—dc22   2007039036

Manufactured in the United States of America
1 2 3 4 5 6 — BP — 14 13 12 11 10 09

Table of Contents

THIS IS THE STORY of how workers build a new school. Their work takes place during one year. All the pictures have the same view of the construction site. But each one shows a different time of year. Lots of things happen during this year. Can you spot them all?

You can follow all the action on the building site as the months pass. The calendar on each right-hand page tells you what month you've reached.

While the work goes on, all sorts of other things are happening. They are not always part of the plan! A few small accidents take place. Animals and children come and go. There's always something new to find!

As you read, look for people who appear every month. For example, someone always seems to be chasing a dog. And one worker is always eating. Think about what stories these people might tell about the construction site.

Can you
find . . .

an old sink?

Before workers can build the new school, they must tear down an old building on the site. This work is called demolition. A crane swings a heavy metal ball at the walls. Bricks from the walls crash to the ground. A special claw grabs window frames and water pipes. Bulldozers clear away the broken-up bits, or rubble.

a hose?

a heavy saw?

A few weeks later, bulldozers clear away the last of the rubble. Workers cut up old metal beams. To do this work, they use special tools. Bulldozers also dig narrow paths called trenches. This is where the new building's foundation will be. The foundation is the building's base. Earthmovers scoop the dirt into dump trucks to be taken away. The digging has uncovered a few surprises. One builder finds an old pillar. Other workers spot a fossil (the remains of an ancient animal).

February

Demolition

Digging the foundation

Pumping concrete

Placing the floors

Setting the roof timbers

Adding roof tiles

Building a street

Painting the walls

Can you find . . .

a worker spreading concrete?

a builder's plans?

The time has come to put in the foundation. A concrete mixer pours a building material called concrete into a machine. The machine pumps concrete into the foundation. When the concrete dries, it becomes very hard. At the same time, a crane rises high above the action. It will carry supplies to the upper floors. Trucks deliver bricks and beams for the new school.

TOILET

March

Demolition

Digging the foundation

Pumping concrete

Placing the floors

Setting the roof timbers

Adding roof tiles

Building a street

Painting the walls

an electric drill?

a pickax?

a dog?

a bucket?

The building is taking shape. Trucks bring slabs to make the floors. A crane lowers the floor slabs in place. Workers are also building the frame of the school. They use a special type of concrete. It makes the building extra strong. Workers set up wooden platforms so they can finish the building's outside. As the building gets taller, the platforms get taller too.

May

Demolition

Digging the foundation

Pumping concrete

Placing the floors

Setting the roof timbers

Adding roof tiles

Building a street

Painting the walls

Can you find . . .

a round saw?

a concrete mixer?

a toolbox?

a wheelbarrow?

The frame of the building is finished. The builders start laying bricks. They are supposed to leave spaces for the windows. But one window has been bricked in! Trucks bring in long pieces of wood called timbers. The timbers are for the roof. The crane lifts the pieces to the top of the building. Workers hammer them into place.

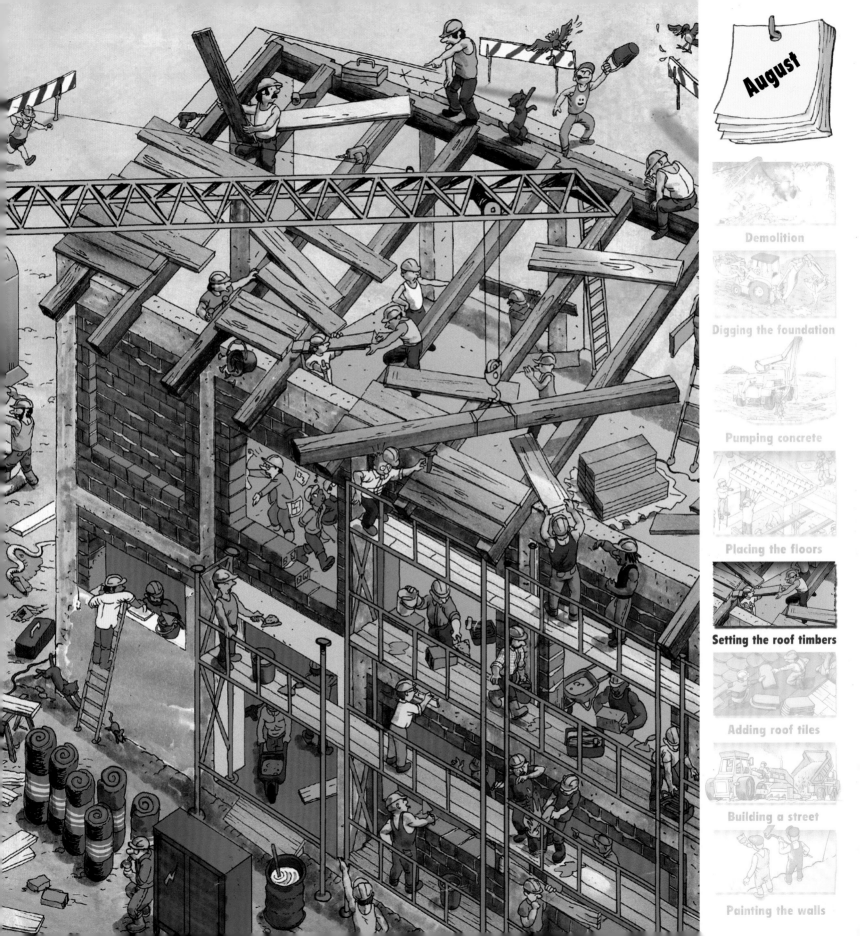

August

Demolition

Digging the foundation

Pumping concrete

Placing the floors

Setting the roof timbers

Adding roof tiles

Building a street

Painting the walls

Can you
find . . .

bags of
cement?

a worker fitting a
window frame?

a shovel?

a movable
toilet?

The roof is nearly done. The roofers unroll thick paper called felt. They nail it to the timbers. Then they put roof tiles on top of the paper. Some builders fit window frames into the spaces left in the walls. A small crane brings sheets of glass to the builders standing on the platforms. At the same time, a bulldozer and an earthmover have come back. They are starting to build the street that will lead to the school.

October

Demolition

Digging the foundation

Pumping concrete

Placing the floors

Setting the roof timbers

Adding roof tiles

Building a street

Painting the walls

Can you
find . . .

a plumber?

a worker
planting a tree?

a plasterer?

sleeping workers?

The outside of the building and the street are nearly finished. Trucks carrying hot tar arrive. They tip the tar onto a machine that spreads it smoothly on the road. A roller presses the tar flat. But what's going on inside the building? To help you see, the picture has part of the roof and front wall taken away. A lot of new workers are on the site. Plasterers coat the brick walls with plaster. Electricians wire the school. Plumbers put in water pipes. Only a few small accidents happen! Soon the school has smooth walls, electric wiring, and running water.

November

Demolition

Digging the foundation

Pumping concrete

Placing the floors

Setting the roof timbers

Adding roof tiles

Building a street

Painting the walls

Can you find . . .

a blackboard?

a worker painting a white line?

a man with a camera?

a school clock?

a paintbrush?

The picture again shows what's going on inside and outside. The school is nearly ready to open. Workers are busy painting the walls. Movers bring in new desks. Builders put the doors on closets. Outside, gardeners have planted trees and shrubs. A worker paints a white line down the middle of the new street. Other workers add a crosswalk. And people are curious! A TV crew rushes to be the first to talk to the principal. They want to know what he thinks of his brand-new school. A soccer team and some students stop by. The new school will open next year.

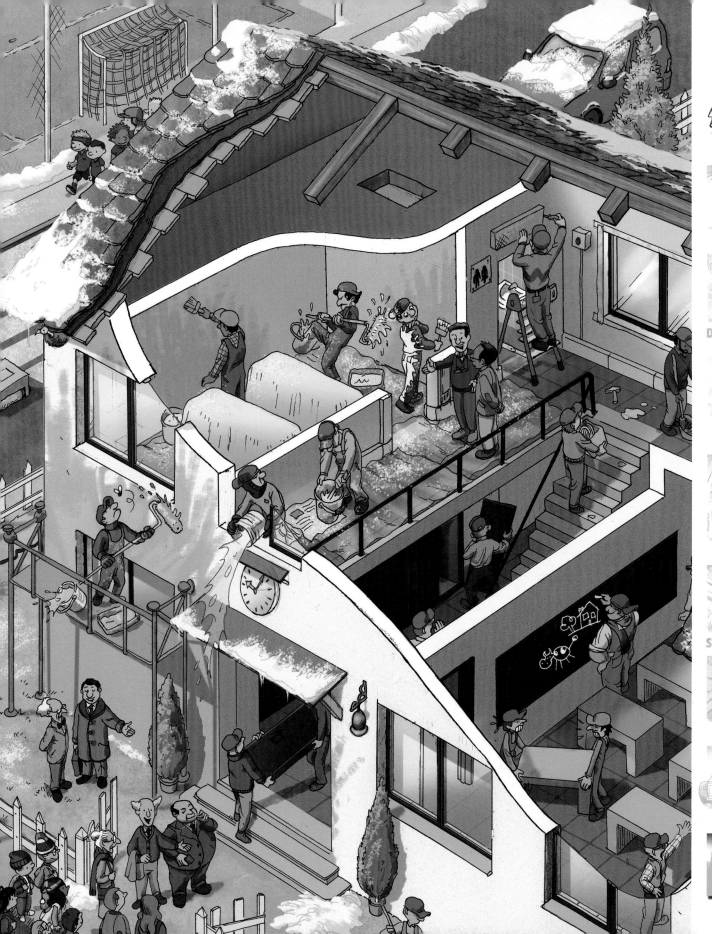

Demolition

Digging the foundation

Pumping concrete

Placing the floors

Setting the roof timbers

Adding roof tiles

Building a street

Painting the walls

Glossary

bulldozer: a powerful tractor that can move dirt and rocks

concrete: a building material made from sand, rocks, cement, and water

demolition: knocking down something

earthmover: a machine that can dig up and move dirt

fossil: the hardened remains of an ancient animal or plant

foundation: the solid base on which a building is built

plaster: a material made of sand, water, and lime that is smoothed on walls

rubble: broken bricks and stones

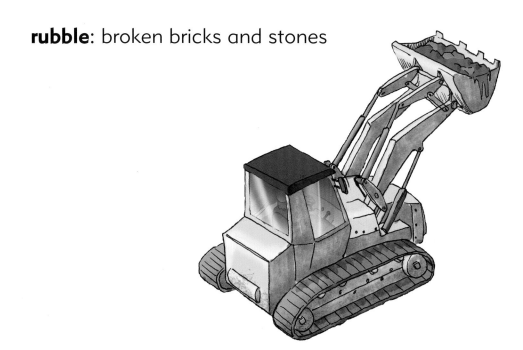

Learn More about Construction

Books

Brill, Marlene Targ. *Concrete Mixers*. Minneapolis: Lerner Publications Company, 2007.

Bullard, Lisa. *Cranes*. Minneapolis: Lerner Publications Company, 2007.

Hayward, Linda. *A Day in a Life of a Builder*. New York: DK Children, 2001.

Hill, Lee Sullivan. *Earthmovers*. Minneapolis: Lerner Publications Company, 2003.

Jango-Cohen, Judith. *Dump Trucks*. Minneapolis: Lerner Publications Company, 2003.

Kilby, Don. *At a Construction Site*. Tonawanda, NY: Kids Can Press, 2006.

Liebman, Dan. *I Want to Be a Builder*. Richmond Hill, ON: Firefly Books, 2003.

Nelson, Robin. From *Tree to House*. Minneapolis: Lerner Publications Company, 2004.

Taus-Bolstad, Stacy. *From Clay to Bricks*. Minneapolis: Lerner Publications Company, 2003.

Zemlicka, Shannon. *From Rock to Road*. Minneapolis: Lerner Publications Company, 2004.

Websites

Bob the Builder
http://www.bobthebuilder.com
The official website of Bob the Builder offers games, puzzles, and more for kid builders.

Kikki's Workshop
http://www.kenkenkikki.jp/e_index2.html
This website is all about the machines used in building. It has pictures, games, pages to color, and more.

A Closer Look

This book has a lot to find. Did you see people who showed up again and again? Think about what these people did and saw during the year. If these people kept journals, what would they write? A journal is a book with blank pages where people write down their thoughts. Have you ever kept a journal? What did you write about?

Try making a journal for one of the characters in this book. You will need a pencil and a piece of paper. Choose your character. Give your character a name. Write the name of the month at the top of the page. Underneath, write about the character's life during that month. Pretend you are the character. What kind of work are you doing? Is your work hard or easy? Why? What have you noticed about the new school? Have you seen anything surprising at work? What? What do you hope to do next month?

Don't worry if you don't know how to spell every word. You can ask a parent or teacher for help if you need to. And be creative!

Index